Nick Kyrgios: The Inspiring Story of One of Tennis' Stars

An Unauthorized Biography

By: Clayton Geoffreys

Table of Contents

Foreword

When thinking of recent Australian tennis stars, it doesn't take long before Nick Kyrgios' name comes to mind. Kyrgios has accomplished a lot in his tennis career, having reached eleven finals at the time of this writing, including a 2022 Wimbledon Championships final. Kyrgios is a polarizing player. To some, he is wildly entertaining and to others, he can be perceived as over the top in his on court antics. Wherever you fall in the spectrum of Nick Kyrgios fan, there's no denying that Kyrgios is great at his craft. Thank you for purchasing *Nick Kyrgios: The Inspiring Story of One of Tennis' Stars*. In this unauthorized biography, we will learn Nick Kyrgios' incredible life story and impact on the game of tennis. Hope you enjoy and if you do, please do not forget to leave a review!

Also, check out my website to join my exclusive list where I let you know about my latest books. To thank you for your purchase, I'll gift you free copies of some of my other books at **claytongeoffreys.com/goodies**.

Or, if you don't like typing, scan the QR code here to go there directly.

Cheers,

Clayton Geoffreys

Visit me at www.claytongeoffreys.com

Introduction

For virtually the entire 21st century, men's professional tennis has been dominated by three larger-than-life players. These players have defined an era and rewritten the record books, ultimately transcending tennis to become legends of world sport.

Roger Federer was the first of these figures to emerge; the Swiss phenom was so graceful and dominant that he has frequently been referred to as the "maestro" of tennis. Then came Rafael Nadal, the indomitable rival who rose to Federer's level and lorded his authority over clay courts to an almost unfathomable degree. And then there was Novak Djokovic, the tireless challenger who would ultimately outlast both Federer and Nadal and, against all odds, claim most of their records as his own.

These three men have so thoroughly controlled men's tennis for the last 20 years that they have eclipsed some extraordinarily talented players in the process.

Many talented competitors who might have reached the heights of the sport were it not for the "Big Three" have instead spent their careers struggling to win even one or two prestigious titles.

At the same time, however, the dominance of the Big Three also caused many in the tennis world to keep a close eye out for emerging players who *might* have had it in them to ascend toward the top of the sport. This is how a brash young Australian named Nick Kyrgios first came to the attention of the tennis world.

Kyrgios was by no means the first young player the tennis world turned to hoping for a fresh challenger to the Big Three. A common trend among tennis fans, writers, and analysts to attempt to identify the "next big thing" started around 2007 when a handful of extremely promising young talents began to emerge.

First among those talents was Jo-Wilfried Tsonga, an athletic French player who had won the Junior U.S. Open in 2003 and stormed the Australian Open final in

2008 in just his second year on the pro tour. Then came Kei Nishikori, who won his first ATP title at 19 years of age on the way to becoming the ATP Newcomer of the Year in 2008. That same year, Australia's Bernard Tomic and Bulgaria's Grigor Dimitrov won three of the four junior grand slams. Both were touted as players with the potential to challenge the very best players on the ATP Tour.

When Nick Kyrgios arrived on the tennis world's radar a few years later, circumstances were a little different. Tsonga, Nishikori, and Dimitrov had all become very good professional players. It had also become apparent, though, that the Big Three remained on their own tier, seemingly invincible, with the ultra-talented but oft-injured Andy Murray being the only regular challenger to their continued supremacy.

In that respect, it had become all the more difficult to view up-and-coming players as threats to the top of the ATP ranks. As good as they were, Tsonga, Nishikori, and Dimitrov had all fallen a bit short. On the other hand, the tennis world was as eager as ever to see a new champion emerge.

Nick Kyrgios fit the bill in that he seemed not only talented, but *different*. The Australian climbed up the junior ranks in the late 2000s and early 2010s relying on a loose, athletic, and frankly, uncommon style. He had a fiery, independent attitude and the game to back it up, and perhaps even seemed like a high-level athlete who had somehow landed in the wrong sport. Young Kyrgios was not concerned with modeling his playing style after the greats who had come before him, nor was he particularly preoccupied with the etiquette of tennis. He was more improvisational, and for that reason, he stood out.

Whether Kyrgios should ever have been tabbed as another "next big thing" in men's tennis is debatable. He commanded attention, and he certainly had the talent and athleticism to match the hype. At the same time, however, it was clear early on that his discipline was somewhat lacking. On top of that, the tennis world had already placed an unfair burden of expectations on several talented young players before him. As tempting as it was to look at Kyrgios and see a future multi-time Grand Slam champion, it might not have been *reasonable* to do so.

At the time of this writing, Nick Kyrgios is in the twilight of his career. To date, he has fallen a bit short of some of the lofty expectations others had placed on his shoulders. But the way in which his career has played out has actually turned him into one of the most relatable tennis stars of the Big Three era.

Here is a player whose pure talent and ability may well have placed him in the company of legends, but whose naked flaws kept him on a more human level. On any given day, Kyrgios could look like a mythical figure sent to disrupt the untouchable dominance of the Big Three. The very next day, though, he could look like any one of us mere mortals having a frustrating day on the local courts.

Nick Kyrgios may never have become the next big thing on tour, but frankly, there isn't much evidence that that was even what he aspired to be. In being true to himself, for better or worse, he still managed to become a highly successful professional and one of the most unique and interesting players professional tennis has seen in decades.

Chapter 1: Childhood and Early Life

Nick Kyrgios was born on April 27, 1995, in Canberra, Australia. His father Giorgos (or "George") is a house painter of Greek origin, and his mother Norlaila (nicknamed "Nill") is a computer engineer who was born into Malaysian royalty. Nick also has two older siblings, a sister named Halimah who now works as a theater and voice coach in Hong Kong, and a brother named Christos who is a fitness trainer.

An extensive profile of Nick Kyrgios published at *ESPN* in 2023 revealed that, in his youth, Nick would "shadow" his older siblings around the house.[i] The family was described as "tight-knit," which was essential to Nick's childhood. The fact that Nill dealt with a variety of health issues made Nick anxious at home. The fact that he was of a darker complexion than most people in Canberra and also struggled with his weight made it hard for him to fit in outside of the house. With these stress factors weighing on his young shoulders, Nick stayed close to his family.

He also turned to sports. While not a great deal has been made public about the specifics of Nick's earliest training routines, we know that he started to play tennis with his mother as early as age six. In the Netflix documentary *Break Point,* which focused its first episode on Kyrgios, his mother recalled that he had had his first actual lessons at age seven.[ii] Around the same time, Nick also delved into basketball, which has often been characterized (including by Nick himself) as his true love.

Unlike some other prodigious talents in the tennis world, Nick was not placed in the care of a high-profile coach or shipped off to an academy to pursue professional aspirations. Nevertheless, it is clear that he felt an inherent pressure to perform and live up to his potential quite early. In the aforementioned profile, Nill was quoted describing Nick as an emotional child.

She recalled once seeing her son toss his lunch box and racket before bursting into tears over a match loss. He was only eight years old.

Over the next few years, Nick would pursue both tennis and basketball. His body filled out well and his significant natural athleticism became apparent. Standing more than 6' tall in his early teenage years, Nick conceivably had a chance to pursue a career in either of his main sports. And to hear him tell it, he may well have preferred basketball. When he was 14, however, his parents made the decision for him.

In that same *ESPN* write-up, Nill Kyrgios recalled that it had become too difficult to balance Nick's education, tennis training, and basketball schedule all at the same time. Nick was attending Radford College, an independent school in Bruce, while trying to juggle both sports. It had reached the point, though, that he could only make it to basketball games but had to skip practices. As Nill remembered it, other parents would question why Nick was getting playing time in basketball games when he was not even attending training.

Faced with this time management dilemma, George and Nill weighed their options. They had witnessed Australian players walk the path to professional tennis before, but professional basketball seemed to be a more distant, opaque proposition. So, when Nick was 14, his father simply informed him that the family would be dropping basketball to "put everything into tennis."

"He pretty much snatched the dream away from me," Nick has said about that decision in the years since. He acknowledged, however, that he was a "fair bit better at tennis." That said, his childhood best friend and later professional manager Daniel Horsfall has also described him as having been a "freak basketball player."

We will never know just how far Nick Kyrgios might have taken his early basketball dream. He listened to his parents on that day back in 2009 and accepted the idea of shifting his athletic focus solely to tennis. By that time, he had already begun to dip his toes into official junior tennis competition. And as he progressed further into his teenage years, he would become a mainstay on the junior circuit as well as one of the most promising young tennis talents in the entire world.

Chapter 2: Junior Career

For up-and-coming tennis players with professional aspirations, there is a sort of international system of amateur tournaments. This is organized by the International Tennis Federation (ITF), and is commonly referred to as the junior circuit. Players can begin competing on this circuit once they turn 13 and can continue to enter ITF events through the full season during which they turn 18.

To some degree, the point of the ITF Junior Circuit is to provide a version of the ATP Tour for young players to get used to. Professional tennis involves travel like no other sport in the world, and while the junior circuit is not quite as intensive as the ATP Tour, it can give young players practice managing their schedules and incorporating travel into their training and preparation routines. That said, junior tennis can also provide some younger players with a chance to face elite competition even if they are not embarking on worldwide travels just yet. So it was with Nick Kyrgios, who spent his earliest days in the junior circuit staying relatively close to home.

Those early days started in the fall of 2008 and progressed into the spring of 2009 as young Kyrgios approached his 14th birthday. ITF junior events are organized by "grades," with Grade A representing the most prestigious competitions, Grade B representing regional championship tournaments, and Grade C designated for international team competition; beneath these are Grades 1 through 5, with 1 typically involving more advanced players and 5 the youngest or least advanced.

Nick started off by entering two Grade 4 tournaments in Australia. He then entered the Grade 5 Waikato Bays ITF Tournament in Hamilton, New Zealand, and earned his first win in singles as well as three doubles matches playing alongside James Frawley. By the end of the 2009 season, Kyrgios had amassed an 8-7 record in singles playing exclusively Grade 4 and 5 events.

At the outset of the 2010 season, Nick ramped up his competition significantly. He played in the Grade 1 Loy Yang Traralgon International in Traralgon, Australia, and then played in the qualifying draw of the Australian Open Junior Championships. This earned him valuable match experience, after which he drifted back to Grade 4 events. Kyrgios then won his first ITF junior title at the Grade 4 Air Pacific South Pacific Open Junior Championships in Lautoka, Fiji, in July. That would be his only title for the season, but he would ultimately wrap up 2010 with an impressive 23-13 record having played in a handful of higher-grade tournaments.

Early in 2011, Nick earned a spot in the main draw of the Australian Open Junior Championships and won consecutive matches before losing in the third round. That summer, soon after his 16th birthday, he won two qualifying matches to gain entry to the main draw at the Junior Championships, Wimbledon, for the first time. He then fell in the first round to Great Britain's Liam Broady, who would go on to be a mainstay on the ATP Tour.

Kyrgios would not play the Junior U.S. Open that year, but in the fall, he would notch his most significant victories yet to win the Grade 2 Dunlop Japan Open Junior Championships. The following month, he also claimed a doubles title at the Grade B Seogwipo Closed International Junior Tennis Championships in Japan, partnering once again with James Frawley.

Despite having had a few years dabbling in junior competition already, it was in 2012 that Kyrgios shifted his perspective toward a true pursuit of professional tennis. As he himself put it in the *Break Point* episode "The Maverick," "I didn't really know how good I was … When I was about 17 I finally just had a growth spurt. All of a sudden, I started sliding and moving … I was like, 'I've been blessed.' And then things got quite serious."[ii]

That seriousness during Kyrgios's age-17 season manifested in a busier schedule, combining junior competitions with occasional forays into professional events. On the junior calendar, he kept his focus largely on high-grade tournaments and had considerable success.

Nick made the main draws at the Australian Open Junior Championships and Roland Garros Junior French Championships (the junior French Open), winning one singles match at each event. He also won the Roland Garros Junior French Championships in doubles alongside fellow Australian Andrew Harris. In July, his game jumped to another level as he made a quarter-final run in the Junior Championships, Wimbledon singles, won the event with Harris in doubles, and then seized a Grade 1 singles title at the Canadian Open Junior Championships.

Kyrgios closed out the 2012 season with a quarter-final run at the U.S. Open Junior Tennis Championships (making the final in the doubles) and a Grade A tournament win at the World Super Junior Tennis Championships in Osaka, Japan.

Following this title, the young Australian told reporters, "It was overwhelming, just because there was a lot of expectation. I was just glad to get the job done."[iii]

That expectation reflected the fact that Kyrgios had been on a steady rise up the junior ranks for about a year and a half at that point. With the Grade A win in Osaka, he solidified himself as the #4 junior player in the world to end the year.

2013 marked Nick Kyrgios's age-18 season, and the last year in which he could compete in the junior ranks. By that point, he was already playing some professional matches and was recognized as an emerging talent on the fringes of the ATP Tour. Still, he saw fit to play in some of the bigger junior events throughout the first half of the year.

Kyrgios picked up right where he left off in Osaka, winning the title at the Grade 1 AGL Loy Yang Traralgon International. That win secured the #1 junior ranking for Kyrgios. He then won his first and only singles Grand Slam as a junior by breezing through the Australian Open Junior Championships field without dropping a set; he beat his close friend and doubles partner Thanasi Kokkinakis, also representing Australia, in the final.

Kyrgios had less luck at the Roland Garros Junior French Championships, where he won just one match before losing to future top-10 ATP pro Karen Khachanov. He then triumphed at the grass-court Grade 1 AEGON Junior International tournament in Roehampton, Great Britain, beating future tour-level stars Daniil Medvedev, Borna Coric, and Alexander Zverev along the way. Nick would then bring his junior career to a close at the Junior Championships, Wimbledon, where he lost in the third round in singles but won the doubles with Kokkinakis.

All in all, it had been a sensational junior career for Kyrgios. From playing Grade 4 and Grade 5 events in Oceania as a 13-year-old who was still harboring basketball ambitions, he had grown into the worldwide #1 junior tennis player. He had won a junior grand slam in singles and three more in doubles.

Earlier in the season when Kyrgios won the Junior Australian Open, his then-coach Des Tyson had cautioned him that a junior slam did not guarantee ATP Tour success.

"It's a good start and a good step, but there's a lot of work to be done yet," he said, adding, "It's not going to happen overnight, it could take maybe four or five years to make that transition."[iv]

These were wise words, rooted in the simple fact that not all successful juniors even end up sustaining careers on the senior tour. At the same time, though, Nick Kyrgios did not seem ordinary. At his best, he was already proving to be a unique showman and a talent that fans could not look away from. As such, there were high expectations as soon as he committed fully to the pro tour. Case in point—the very article that published those quotes from Des Tyson ignored the coach's well-reasoned caution, declaring in its headline that Kyrgios was "ready to be a star."

Chapter 3: Professional Career

Easing into the ATP Tour

Part of the reason for the star-in-waiting perception surrounding Nick Kyrgios was that he had already gained some professional tour-level experience before he wrapped up his time in the juniors. This experience came in multiple forms.

First, there were ITF Futures events, which function almost as a semi-professional tier where up-and-coming players can compete for points toward their ATP rankings. Additionally, there were ATP Challenger tournaments, where professional players of all ages play year-round to boost their rankings in the hopes of easing their paths to ATP Tour events. And on top of Futures and Challenger competitions, Kyrgios had a few early forays into tour-level tennis as well.

Those forays began at the 2012 Australian Open when Kyrgios was still only 17 years old. He was able to enter the tournament's qualifying draw without an ATP ranking of his own and even won the opening set against France's Mathieu Rodrigues, the world #215. Kyrgios lost the next two sets and was thus eliminated from qualifying but gained valuable experience in the effort.

Throughout the remainder of the 2012 season, Kyrgios mixed a number of ITF Futures events into his schedule between junior tournaments. He went 9-7 in total across these events, and in doing so, crept into the top 900 in the ATP rankings before he had, strictly speaking, "turned pro."

Before his run in the Australian Open Junior Championships in 2013, Kyrgios entered the qualifying draw of a tour-level tournament in Brisbane. This was an ATP 250 event, which is the smallest and least prestigious designation among ATP tournaments. The next level up is an ATP 500, followed by a Masters 1000 and then a Grand Slam. In this instance,

Kyrgios played in the qualifying draw but lost in the first round to fellow Aussie James Duckworth. Kyrgios actually tried to qualify for the main Australian Open draw as well, but lost in the opening round of qualifying there, too, to world #255 Bradley Klahn.

Kyrgios then progressed to a number of strong results as the early portion of the 2013 season rolled along. He reached the semi-final of a Challenger tournament in Adelaide in the first week of February and then won another Challenger in Sydney at the end of the month. He followed these performances with three Futures tournaments in China, reaching a semi-final in the first and a final in the second before winning the third.

After this run of spring Challenger and Futures tournaments, Kyrgios earned a surprise wild card spot in the main draw of the 2013 French Open. He was the youngest player in the draw just a few weeks past his 18th birthday and only got a spot because John

Millman, another Australian player, had to withdraw with an injury. Kyrgios took advantage of the opportunity with a stirring 7-6, 7-6, 7-6 win over world #52 Radek Stepanek.

Of this first win in a Grand Slam main draw, Kyrgios said that it "felt about 10 times better than the championship point at the junior Australian Open."[v] He expressed gratitude to everyone who had helped him reach that point and said he could not fully describe the feeling.

Stepanek, meanwhile, was graceful in defeat at the hands of the athletic Australian. He echoed coach Des Tyson's sentiment that a good career in juniors did not guarantee success but stated that Kyrgios would have "a chance" thanks to his talent and big serve.

Kyrgios lost in the second round at Roland Garros to then-#11 Marin Cilic in straight sets. Nevertheless, he emerged from the French Open having raised his own ranking up to 213th in the world.

After a quick stop at a Challenger in Nottingham and his final run in the Junior Championships, Wimbledon, Kyrgios got another whiff of a Grand Slam main draw. He traveled to New York to compete in qualifying for the U.S. Open and won three matches to secure a spot in the draw. There, he faced world #4 David Ferrer and lost 5-7, 3-6, 2-6.

After winning a match for the Australian team in a Davis Cup tie with Poland and playing two more Challengers, Kyrgios's transition season came to an end. He had raised his ranking to 182nd in the world without having played in an ATP Tour main draw, save for at two Grand Slams.

A Breakthrough at Wimbledon

As of the beginning of the 2014 season, Nick Kyrgios was no longer eligible for junior events. He was entering his age-19 season and facing a full professional schedule for the first time. This started at the Australian Open in Melbourne, where Kyrgios was into the main draw without having to qualify. He defeated #81 Benjamin Becker in his first match and then battled #28 Benoit Paire in a second-round contest that captivated the tennis world.

Though Kyrgios ultimately struggled with cramps and lost to Paire by a score of 7-6, 7-6, 4-6, 2-6, 2-6, he had made a loud statement with his big serves, athletic court coverage, and fluid shot-making. *Sports Illustrated* aptly called the young Aussie's play "precocious" in its recap and cited excited social media reactions from the likes of tennis pro Victoria Azarenka and one-time Roger Federer coach Paul Annacone.[vi] Everyone who watched seemed to have been impressed by Kyrgios's talent. As for the player himself, he took his loss well. Kyrgios thanked the crowd for its energy and called it an honor to have played at Margaret Court Arena.

Kyrgios next competed for Australia in a Davis Cup matchup with France. This did not go particularly well for the Aussies, but the young star got an opportunity to play against a top-10 opponent in Richard Gasquet and an ultra-athletic foe in Gael Monfils. He lost both matches but made them competitive, nonetheless.

From there, Kyrgios traveled to the U.S. to play an ATP 250 in Memphis, where he lost in the first round. Then, rather than continue on the U.S. hard-court circuit, he took to a string of smaller clay-court events. These gave him an opportunity to both boost his ranking and warm up for Roland-Garros.

Kyrgios won consecutive clay-court Challengers in Sarasota and Savannah and, along the way, beat a handful of opponents who were either perennial top-100 players or would be in the future. These included Americans Donald Young and Jack Sock, Serbian Filip Krajinovic, and Japan's Yoshihito Nishioka. Kyrgios also beat his friend Thanasi Kokkinakis in the opening round in Savannah.

His ranking now up to #159, Kyrgios ventured to Europe for another clay challenger in Heilbronn, Germany, where he lost in the opening round. He then attempted to qualify for an ATP 250 in Dusseldorf but was beaten in his second qualifying match by countryman Jason Kubler, who was actually ranked well beneath him. To cap off the clay-court season, Kyrgios made his way into the main draw at the French Open. He lost in straight sets to Canadian Milos Raonic, another player who had been hyped with "next big thing" status and who had climbed to 9th in the world.

Next up was the summer grass-court swing. Kyrgios started off at a Challenger in Nottingham but lost in the first round to another Australian named John-Patrick Smith. At a subsequent Challenger event in Nottingham, however (aptly known as Nottingham-2), Kyrgios suddenly rattled off a nine-match winning streak. He prevailed in three qualifying rounds before bullying his way through a field of rising pros that included the UK's Kyle Edmund, Filip Krajinovic, and, in the final, Australia's Sam Groth. The tournament win sent Kyrgios to Wimbledon with a career-high ranking of 144th in the world.

At Wimbledon, Kyrgios would make an emphatic statement that the excitement about his talent had not been overblown. He started off by winning a 7-6, 7-6, 6-7, 6-2 battle with France's Stephane Robert, the 78th-ranked player in the world. Then, he faced 13-seed Richard Gasquet, who had previously beaten him in Davis Cup competition. Kyrgios lost the first two sets 3-6, 6-7 but rallied to win the next three 6-4, 7-5, and 10-8, saving a stunning nine match points to do it.

Expressing that he was proud of himself after the match, Nick stated that his goal was to become the #1 player in the world.[vii] As for Gasquet, the talented French player simply said, "He is a very talented player and today he was a beast."

Kyrgios lost another opening set in his third-round match against the Czech Republic's Jiri Vesely. He then rallied to win in four and advance to the Round of 16. At that stage, the rising Aussie was matched up against world #1 Rafael Nadal. They were two of the most athletic players on tour, but Nadal was a seasoned, multi-time Slam champion while Kyrgios was only just emerging. They traded sets to open the match before Kyrgios won a critical third-set tiebreak. From there, he was able to gain some separation and pull off a stunning upset, 7-6, 5-7, 7-6, 6-3.

"You've got to believe you can win the match from the start," Kyrgios said of the upset that would define his early career.[viii] He then once again thanked the people who'd helped him get to this point, saying, "They get me over the line."

Looking at the match from more of a big-picture standpoint, former star and regular commentator John McEnroe said, simply, "We're watching a young boy turn into a man. We have a new star on our hands in the tennis world."

In the ensuing quarter-final round, Kyrgios got off to a good start against Milos Raonic, who had knocked him out of the French Open in the first round. The Aussie won the first set in a tiebreak but then ran out of gas, ultimately losing 7-6, 2-6, 4-6, 6-7 to the big Canadian. Nevertheless, Kyrgios had stolen the show at the 2014 Wimbledon Championships. He had also risen not only into the top 100 in the world rankings for the first time, but all the way up to #70.

Kyrgios next competed at the Toronto Masters 1000 in early August. He upset world #30 Santiago Giraldo in the first round to earn his first-ever chance to face Great Britain's Andy Murray, whom many considered to be the fourth-best player in the world behind the vaunted "Big Three" of Federer, Nadal, and Djokovic. Kyrgios fell 2-6, 2-6.

Despite that result, the young Aussie boosted his ranking another 10 spots and earned a main-draw entry at the U.S. Open in New York. He won a very competitive opening-round match over #23 Mikhail Youzhny and then upset Italy's Andreas Seppi, the world #49, in straight sets. That took Kyrgios into the Round of 32, where he was stopped by 16-seed Tommy Robredo.

Kyrgios emerged from the U.S. Open on the cusp of the top 50. He next played in a Davis Cup clash with Uzbekistan, beating #55 Denis Istomin and #736 Sanjar Fayziev in his singles matches. He then traveled to Kuala Lumpur for an ATP 250 and lost to fellow Australian Marinko Matosevic in the first round. This would conclude his season. Kyrgios declined to play additional tournaments to avoid exhausting himself in his first full year on the pro tour.

With a year-end ranking of 52nd in the world and a Wimbledon quarter-final under his belt, the 19-year-old had fully arrived as a young player with genuine star potential. Indeed, the victory over Nadal at Wimbledon had raised the already-lofty expectations surrounding him and earned him worldwide recognition.

Said Kyrgios in Netflix's *Break Point*, "I went from no one knowing who I was to people camping outside my house. That match changed everything. Everything. From that day forth, the expectation for me to be the next big thing was massive."[ii]

Strength at Slams

Nick Kyrgios started the 2015 season at an ATP 250 in Sydney, a common stop for players on their way to the Australian Open. He was, by that point, ranked 50th in the world but lost his opening match to world #42 Jerzy Janowicz of Poland. This dropped Kyrgios back down to #53, though it did nothing to stop him from comfortably earning a spot in the Australian Open main draw.

Back in Melbourne for his home Grand Slam, Kyrgios faced a stiff opening-round test against a determined Federico Delbonis, the world #62. In the end, the aggressive young Aussie prevailed in a back-and-forth affair, 7-6, 3-6, 6-3, 6-7, 6-3. Kyrgios next faced the towering Croatian Ivo Karlovic and toughed out a high-powered match, 7-6, 6-4, 5-7, 6-4. That propelled the 19-year-old into the Round of 32, where he had a slightly easier time with a straight-sets win over #75 Malek Jaziri.

Kyrgios fell behind a set to #46 Andreas Seppi in the Round of 16 before rallying for a grueling five-set win. That put him into his second Grand Slam quarter-final in his last three tries and earned him a second career meeting with Andy Murray. Once again, though, the British champion proved too tricky. Murray won 6-3, 7-6, 6-3.

Both men were gracious after the match. Murray complimented Kyrgios's "exceptional" serve and

Kyrgios stated that Murray was "way too good" for him but that it had been a great experience.[ix] It was the young Australian's first match on Melbourne's iconic Rod Laver Arena court.

What ought to have followed was a run of hard-court tournaments culminating in the United States "Sunshine Double" of Masters 1000 events in Indian Wells, California, and Miami, Florida. However, Nick skipped a portion of this hard-court swing due to a minor back injury and did not take the court again until Indian Wells. There, the now-37th-ranked Australian beat #131 Denis Kudla in the opening round and had #11 Grigor Dimitrov on the ropes in the second. After tweaking an ankle, though, Kyrgios ultimately lost to the smooth-hitting Bulgarian.

Kyrgios skipped the Miami Masters 1000 and then lost in his first match at the ATP 500 in Barcelona to start the clay-court season. Thereafter, he competed in the ATP 250 in Estoril and reached his first final on the pro tour. He did so by beating a tricky lineup of Albert Ramos-Vinolas, Filip Krajinovic, Robin Hasse, and world #64 Pablo Carreno Busta. However, Kyrgios ultimately lost to Richard Gasquet in the final.

This run helped the young Aussie reach #35 in the world heading into the Madrid Masters 1000. He cruised past #66 Daniel Gimeno-Traver in his first match and earned a date against #2 Roger Federer.

This was understandably a big deal for Nick. He had idolized Federer while growing up and had even had the opportunity as a rising young pro in 2014 to train for a week with the Maestro in Switzerland. So, one could have forgiven Kyrgios for being starstruck on this occasion, but instead, he competed well from the start. He lost a narrow first set in a tiebreak but then rallied to beat the Swiss champion in three. It was a shocking result to most watching, although Kyrgios himself did not seem particularly surprised. If anything, he was just relieved he had played as well as he knew he could.

"I think this is definitely the greatest win of my career so far," Kyrgios said after the match.[x] "It doesn't really feel real at the moment. I didn't really feel like I was playing out there. It almost felt like I was watching. It sort of felt similar to that match at Wimbledon I played against Rafa (Nadal)."

Kyrgios put up a fight against big-serving American John Isner in the next round but lost in three sets. He then fell to #13 Feliciano Lopez in the opening round of the Rome Masters 1000 and lost to #42 Dominic Thiem in the Round of 16 at an ATP 250 in Nice.

Despite these early exits, Kyrgios entered the French Open as the 29-seed. It was his first time seeded at a Grand Slam and he made good on it with an opening straight-sets victory over #77 Denis Istomin. Kyrgios next faced an intriguing matchup with Britain's Kyle Edmund but wound up advancing with a walkover as

Edmund withdrew with an injury. In the Round of 32, Kyrgios came up against Andy Murray, who was back up to #3 in the world. Murray won in straight sets, 6-4, 6-2, 6-3.

After a quick stop at the ATP 500 at London's Queen's Club, where he lost to #4 Stan Wawrinka, Nick entered Wimbledon as the tournament's 26-seed. He beat #64 Diego Schwartzman with relative ease in the first round and did the same to Schwartzman's fellow Argentine, #35 Juan Monaco, in the second. Kyrgios then faced #8 Milos Raonic with a berth in the Round of 16 on the line and overcame the Canadian in a tight four-setter.

Kyrgios faced a familiar foe in Richard Gasquet in the Round of 16. Once again, the crafty and tireless Frenchman proved a difficult opponent for him. Using his polished but slightly unorthodox style and corkscrew backhand to offset Kyrgios's power and movement, Gasquet prevailed 7-5, 6-1, 6-7, 7-6.

After a loss to #115 Aleksandr Nedovyesov in an Australian Davis Cup contest with Kazakhstan, Kyrgios embarked on the North American hard-court swing. He reached the Round of 16 at the Masters 1000 in Montreal with impressive wins over #38 Fernando Verdasco and #5 Stan Wawrinka, but then fell to #12 John Isner.

At the ensuing Masters 1000 in Cincinnati and then the U.S. Open, Kyrgios had a bit of bad fortune in the draws. He was matched up with Richard Gasquet in the first round in Cincinnati and lost 2-6, 1-6. Then, despite a 37th ranking that would often have resulted in a more favorable draw, he faced #3 Andy Murray to start the U.S. Open. Kyrgios lost 5-7, 3-6, 6-4, 1-6.

The 20-year-old Australian played a handful more tournaments down the stretch, including an ATP 250s in Kuala Lumpur, an ATP 500 in Tokyo, and the Masters 1000 in Shanghai. He went 6-4 across these tournaments, with two of the losses coming to top-20 players Feliciano Lopez and Kei Nishikori.

Overall, it had been an up-and-down season on the pro tour for Kyrgios. His 24-19 record was not quite what some had expected to see from him. However, he had reached his first final on the ATP Tour and had impressively raised his ranking to 30th in the world. And, the U.S. Open notwithstanding, he had played particularly strong tennis in the Grand Slams. In fact, 9 of Kyrgios's 24 wins had come in the Slams. This was an early indication that the young Aussie's fiery nature and ultra-aggressive style was perhaps made for the biggest stages. While his youth showed through for much of the calendar season, he seemed to thrive when the occasion called for drama.

Competing for Titles

Now cemented as a top-50 player trending toward the top-20, Nick Kyrgios pressed forward into his age-21 season. He had had his stumbles in 2015, but his highs had been so spectacular that expectations were as high as ever.

2016
The 2016 season started in tremendous fashion for Kyrgios as he opted to begin at the Hopman Cup. This was a competition that pitted mixed doubles teams representing their countries against each other, and Nick had the honor of suiting up for the Australian "Green Team" alongside Daria Gavrilova (with Aussie legend Lleyton Hewitt and Jarmila Wolfe comprising an Australian "Gold Team").

In a round-robin matchup with Germany, Kyrgios won his singles match over the talented Alexander Zverev and then paired with Gavrilova to defeat Zverev and Sabine Lisicki in doubles. Then, when Australia "Green" faced the British team, Kyrgios finally notched a singles win against Andy Murray before he and Gavrilova got the better of Murray and Heather Watson in doubles.

Following another victory over the French team, Australia "Green" was in the final against Ukraine. Gavrilova won her singles match against Elina Svitolina, meaning that Kyrgios could seal the win if he won his own singles clash with Alexandr Dolgopolov. He did so, 6-3, 6-4, winning the Hopman Cup for Australia and earning his first professional title.

Kyrgios followed this triumph with his first seeded appearance at the Australian Open. He notched a straight-sets win over #68 Pablo Carreno Busta in the first round and then won a tight three-setter over #41 Pablo Cuevas to advance to the Round of 32. The 6-seed Tomas Berdych was waiting there, however, and ended Kyrgios's hopes of a deep run at his home Slam.

Unfazed, Nick took a few weeks off and then traveled to Marseille for an ATP 250 to continue the early hard-court season. He won each of his first two matches against Vasek Pospisil and Teymuraz Gabashvili 6-4,

6-4, and then defeated his early-career nemesis, Richard Gasquet, in a dominant 6-0, 6-4 quarter-final showing. Kyrgios then avenged his Australian Open loss with a 6-4, 6-2 win over Tomas Berdych to reach the final. There, he got past #12 Marin Cilic, who had knocked him out of the previous year's French Open, 6-2, 7-6. It was Kyrgios's very first ATP Tour title.

Kyrgios conceded after the match that he had not expected to win the tournament after having taken a short break following the Australian Open. He had simply followed his racket, however, and kept playing well until he hoisted the trophy. Then, in a charismatic display of some of the good-natured antics fans were growing used to from Kyrgios when he was winning, he had a bit of fun with the French crowd, professing to them in French, "I really like cheese."[xi]

Continuing on the hard-court swing, Kyrgios next made a semi-final run at the ATP 500 in Dubai, beating Berdych again along the way. He lost to #4

Stan Wawrinka in the semis but saw his ranking jump up to #27 for his efforts. This led into the Sunshine Double, where Kyrgios started with a short stay at Indian Wells. He earned a first-round bye but was bested by #49 Albert Ramos-Vinolas in the Round of 64.

The second leg of the Sunshine Double, the Miami Masters 1000, brought out much better tennis from Kyrgios. In the opening rounds, he defeated the once-great Marcos Baghdatis and American Tim Smyczek in straightforward fashion. He then overcame #51 Andrey Kuznetsov after a tricky opening set to reach the quarter-finals, where he eked past Milos Raonic, 6-4, 7-6. Kyrgios was beaten by #6 Kei Nishikori in the semi-finals. But his performance helped him ascend into the top 20 for the first time (at #20 exactly).

It was on to the clay courts next for Kyrgios. He started with a semi-final run at an ATP 250 in Estoril, Portugal. This was an interesting run because while

Kyrgios ultimately lost to #71 Nicolas Almagro, he defeated #40 Borna Coric in the quarters. Coric, incidentally, had been the ATP Newcomer of the Year in 2014 as Kyrgios emerged on the tour. It was notable that the Australian had seemingly gotten out ahead of his Croatian counterpart's development.

At the ensuing Madrid Masters 1000, Kyrgios earned a strong win against #4 Stan Wawrinka in the second round before ultimately falling to Kei Nishikori in the quarter-finals. He then played the follow-up Masters 1000 in Rome, beating #10 Milos Raonic in the second round before losing to Rafael Nadal in the Round of 16.

Kyrgios headed to the 2016 French Open as the #19 player in the world and the tournament's 17-seed. It was his best position yet to start a Grand Slam, even if clay was not necessarily his strongest surface. The young Aussie started the tournament with straight-sets wins over opponents ranked #124 and #123 respectively, but then lost to his rival, Richard Gasquet. The match tilted the head-to-head between the two players to 5-2 in Gasquet's favor.

With the summer schedule quickly progressing to grass courts, Kyrgios ventured to London for the ATP 500 at the Queen's Club. He faced a tough first-round draw and wound up losing to Milos Raonic, then #9 in the world. Nevertheless, Kyrgios's ranking jumped up to 18th on the eve of Wimbledon, where he entered as the tournament's 15-seed.

In the first round, Kyrgios faced Radek Stepanek, whom he had once beaten for his first-ever win in a Grand Slam main draw. He won in four sets but then needed five to get past Jamaica's Dustin Brown in the Round of 64. Kyrgios then won a 6-3, 6-7, 6-3, 6-4 match against #21 Feliciano Lopez to reach the Round of 16. He ran into Andy Murray at that stage, though, and could not get past the Brit. Incidentally, Murray was on his way to his second Wimbledon title.

Kyrgios stayed in the top 20 and next competed at the Toronto Masters 1000. However, he was upset by young Canadian Denis Shapovalov, then the #370 player in the world, in the first round. Following this unexpected early exit, the Australian traveled to Atlanta for an ATP 250. After an opening-round bye, he rattled off wins against American Jared Donaldson, #48 Fernando Verdasco, and #97 Yoshihito Nishioka. He faced #17 John Isner, a major hometown favorite, in the final, but overcame the American with the massive serve for a 7-6, 7-6 win. It was Kyrgios's second ATP title.

Fresh off that Atlanta victory, Nick headed to the Cincinnati Masters 1000 at a new high of 16th in the world. He beat #26 Lucas Pouille to start his stay but then fell to Borna Coric after previously beating the Croatian in Portugal. Despite the loss, however, Kyrgios kept his #16 ranking leading up to the U.S. Open.

The year's final Slam did not go very well for the Aussie. Kyrgios had enjoyed a run of excellent play through most of the spring and summer and managed straight-sets wins over his first two opponents in New York. But he then fell behind 2 sets to 1 against #63 Illya Marchenko in the Round of 32 before having to retire with a hip injury.

Fortunately, the injury was not severe and did not keep Kyrgios off the court for very long. He was able to compete for the Australian Davis Cup team against Slovakia, defeating world #127 Andrej Martin. Then it was off to the Asian hard-court swing, where he had a short stay at the ATP 250 in Chengdu but entered the ATP 500 in Tokyo as the #15 player in the world.

This would prove to be one of Kyrgios's best tournaments to date. He defeated #107 Ryan Harrison, once the great American hope for a new champion, in the first round. He was then given a walkover when Radek Stepanek suffered an injury. Kyrgios crushed

#36 Gilles Muller in the quarter-final and won 6-4, 6-4 over #8 Gael Monfils—perhaps the only player on tour more athletic than Kyrgios—in the semis. He met #14 David Goffin in the final and lost the first set before rallying for a 4-6, 6-3, 7-5 win and a second title in just over three months.

His first ATP 500 title nearly made for a fairytale ending to the 2016 season. However, Kyrgios had one more tournament to play in the form of the Shanghai Masters 1000. He defeated #29 Sam Querrey in the first round but then turned in an utterly baffling performance against #110 Mischa Zverev. Seemingly out of sorts from the start, Kyrgios seemed to abandon his effort, playing so lazily that the umpire actually told him he was being unprofessional and must do better.[xii] It was, unfortunately, the most glaring instance of what would become an occasional problem for the moody Australian. He simply wasn't engaged in the match and he suffered a 3-6, 1-6 loss to end his season as a result.

That was a disappointing conclusion to the season, but it did not take away from what Kyrgios had accomplished on the year. He had gone 39-15, won the Hopman Cup, and seized 3 ATP Tour titles. He had also reached a new career-high ranking of #13 in the world to end the season.

2017
Neglecting to play in Oceanic tune-ups, Nick Kyrgios started the 2017 season as the 14-seed at the Australian Open. He crushed his first opponent 6-1, 6-2, 6-2, and then won the first two sets against veteran Italian Andreas Seppi. The match then turned, however, and Seppi mounted a ferocious comeback to upset Kyrgios in the second round.

Following a brief Davis Cup interlude during which Kyrgios won a singles match against the Czech Republic's Jan Satral, the Aussie headed for the early-season hard courts in the West. He reached the semi-final of the ATP 250 in Marseille before losing to #11

Jo-Wilfried Tsonga. Then, at the ATP 500 in Acapulco, Mexico, he enjoyed an unexpected career highlight when he got the chance to face #2 Novak Djokovic in the quarter-finals.

Kyrgios beat the Serbian champion 7-6, 7-5, joining Dominik Hrbaty and Australian legend Lleyton Hewitt as the only players to have won their first encounters against each member of the "Big Three." *The Guardian's* recap characterized Kyrgios's performance as a "masterclass" and noted that when Hewitt had won his first encounters with Federer, Nadal, and Djokovic, all three had been up-and-coming youngsters. Kyrgios had done it when all three were established multi-Slam champions.[xiii]

Kyrgios then lost to #40 Sam Querrey in the Acapulco semi-finals but had once again made a statement to the tennis world about how well he could play at his best. He headed to the Indian Wells Masters 1000 as the #16 player in the world. He made his best run yet at this particular tournament, holding off fast-rising Alexander Zverev in the Round of 32 and beating Djokovic again in the Round of 16. Nick would have next faced Roger Federer in the quarter-finals. However, he wound up withdrawing from the tournament with a minor illness.

Kyrgios was well enough to return to action for the Miami Masters 1000 and went on an impressive run to the semi-finals. After a first-round bye, he defeated #66 Damir Dzumhur, #21 Ivo Karlovic, #12 David Goffin, and #20 Alexander Zverev. Once again, he was matched up against Federer, and this time he was able to play. The Swiss came out on top, but only in an extremely tight 7-6, 6-7, 7-6 match that, once again, left little doubt about Kyrgios's ceiling.

Before the clay-court season, Kyrgios returned to Australia to play in a Davis Cup tie against the U.S. He won both of his singles matches over #23 John Isner and #25 Sam Querrey to help the Aussies advance through the quarter-final.

Missing a portion of the clay season for this Davis Cup action caused Kyrgios's ranking to drop down to #20 again. From this position, he made a Round of 16 run at the Madrid Masters 1000 before losing to Rafael Nadal. It was a nice tournament for the Aussie, and one that was actually punctuated by his success in the doubles arena. Kyrgios teamed up with American doubles specialist Jack Sock for Madrid and won a few matches to reach the quarter-finals. There, they scored what was a signature doubles win for Kyrgios at the time, upending Bob and Mike Bryan, who had long ruled the world of doubles in parts of the 2000s and 2010s. Kyrgios and Sock fell to the duo of Lukasz Kubot and Marcelo Melo in the next round.

Kyrgios then played flat tennis at the ATP 250 in Lyon, losing to #94 Nicolas Kicker after a first-round bye. Then, at the French Open, Kyrgios won just one match before he was bested by #56 Kevin Anderson of South Africa. All in all, it had been a lackluster year on European clay.

From that point through the next several tournaments, Kyrgios's season took an unfortunate turn. He did not necessarily remain in the slump that had mired his clay-court campaign. However, nagging injuries forced him to withdraw from three tournaments in a row following the French Open: the London Queen's Club ATP 500, Wimbledon, and the ATP 500 in Washington, D.C. The Aussie's ranking fell to 24th heading into the pre-U.S. Open Masters series.

Kyrgios started to right the ship at the Montreal Masters 1000. He defeated #45 Viktor Troicki in the first round and #38 Paolo Lorenzi in the second. But in the Round of 16, he lost for the first time to Alexander Zverev, who had rocketed up to #8 in the rankings.

At the Cincinnati Masters 1000, Kyrgios finally seemed to be back on track. He dispatched #13 David

Goffin, ground out a win over #71 Alexandr Dolgopolov, and then came back from a 4-6 opening set to overcome #44 Ivo Karlovic. In the quarters, Kyrgios banked another victory over then-#2 Rafael Nadal, and in the semi-finals, he beat #31 David Ferrer for the first time. Kyrgios was on the cusp of a first Masters 1000 title but was stopped by #11 Grigor Dimitrov. Nevertheless, it had been a very encouraging tournament performance on the eve of the U.S. Open.

Unfortunately, that encouragement turned out to be baseless, at least in the short term. Bothered by an ailing shoulder, Kyrgios was beaten by fellow Aussie John Millman in the opening round of the U.S. Open. Following the match, he offered some troubling comments revealing that, as *USA Today's* recap put it, he did not "understand where he belongs in the grand scheme of the sport."[xiv]

Speaking about his brief relationship with temporary coach Sebastien Grosjean, Kyrgios suggested that he was not dedicated enough to satisfy the intended mentor. "He probably deserves a player that is probably more dedicated to the game than I am," he said, before shockingly adding, "I'm not dedicated to the game at all."

Sadly, those comments were not just indicative of a moment of despair following a bad loss. They represented a trend that had begun to emerge with Kyrgios. He could look in one tournament like a world-beating athlete capable of dethroning the very best in the game. In the next, he could look like that 14-year-old kid who would have rather played basketball—as if, despite his prodigious talents, he did not want to be on a tennis court in the first place.

Kyrgios next competed in the Davis Cup semi-finals against Belgium, beating #77 Steve Darcis but losing to #12 David Goffin as Australia was eliminated. Then, the Aussie played in another tournament aside from the main tour, taking place in the inaugural Laver Cup.

This was a new tournament organized in part by Roger Federer and designed to pit a "Team Europe" against a "Team World." Representing Team World in the round-robin stage, Kyrgios beat #19 Tomas Berdych but lost to Federer himself.

Still clinging to his place in the top 20, Kyrgios traveled to the ATP 500 in Beijing and found his form once again. He reached the semi-finals dropping just one set and then upset #4 Alexander Zverev in an impressive 6-3, 7-5 showing. He lost the final, 2-6, 1-6, to Rafael Nadal, who was then back to #1 in the world.

For all intents and purposes, that was the end of Nick Kyrgios's 2017 season. He lost to #45 Steve Johnson in the first round at the Shanghai Masters 1000 and then in the second round of the ATP 250 in Antwerp, following a bye.

Despite the ups and downs and some troubling questions concerning his commitment to tennis, Kyrgios had had another productive year. He finished

32-18 and #21 in the world. He had also made it to a Masters final for the first time and had continued to play some of his best tennis against the very best players, not just on tour but in its history.

Struggles with Injury and Discipline

As things unfolded in the following years, it would turn out that Kyrgios's #21 year-end ranking in 2017 would represent a longtime high point. The Australian phenom continued to play eye-catching tennis on a regular basis. But from 2018 through 2021, he would also struggle with frequent injuries as well as with his own discipline and commitment to tennis.

2018

2018 marked Nick Kyrgios's age-23 season, which is worth remembering for perspective. So much had been expected of the young Aussie on the basis of his pure talent and athleticism that the tennis world had grown somewhat impatient with him. It was easy to forget that the player questioning his own commitment in

2017 was only 22 years old and was still maturing as a professional athlete.

The season started at the ATP 250 in Brisbane, where Kyrgios showed up and won the title, beating world #3 Grigor Dimitrov in the semi-finals and American Ryan Harrison in the final. This propped his ranking back up to #17 just before the Australian Open.

In Melbourne, Kyrgios made relatively quick work of his first two opponents, Rogerio Dutra Silva and world #65 Viktor Troicki. He then played an absolute thriller against #15 Jo-Wilfried Tsonga, ultimately prevailing 7-6, 4-6, 7-6, 7-6 against the powerful Frenchman. In the ensuing Round of 16, though, Grigor Dimitrov avenged his Brisbane loss by beating Kyrgios 7-6, 7-6, 4-6, 7-6.

The Aussie next played in a Davis Cup tilt against Germany. He was able to defeat Jan-Lennard Struff but lost a singles battle with #5 Alexander Zverev. Soon thereafter, it became known that Kyrgios had been playing with an injured elbow. This caused him to withdraw from a follow-up tournament at Delray Beach and subsequently spoiled much of the first half of his season.

Kyrgios skipped the Indian Wells Masters 1000 before giving it a go at the Miami Masters 1000. He reached the Round of 16 before succumbing to Zverev once more. He subsequently played just one tournament throughout the clay-court season, missing the French Open entirely.

Back to full strength as the grass-court campaign got underway, Kyrgios entered the ATP 250 in Stuttgart as the #24 player in the world. He enjoyed a bye and won two matches before he was bested in three sets by Roger Federer. In the ATP 500 at the London Queen's Club, Kyrgios enjoyed a personal highlight when he defeated Andy Murray for the first time—albeit a version of Murray who was on the comeback trail from injury. That match happened in the first round and was followed by promising Kyrgios wins over #17 Kyle Edmund and #37 Feliciano Lopez. The Aussie fell to #6 Marin Cilic in the semi-finals, however.

Kyrgios then headed to Wimbledon in strong form, particularly given how much the elbow injury had bothered him in the spring. He lasted only three rounds at the All-England Club, however, losing to #28 Kei Nishikori in the Round of 32.

Starting the summer hard-court swing at the ATP 250 in Atlanta, Kyrgios had a first-round bye before dispatching America's Noah Rubin in the Round of 16. He next faced #73 Cameron Norrie in the quarter-final and wound up in an unexpectedly hostile situation.

Struggling with a hip injury, Nick seemed to throw in the towel, as he had occasionally been accused of doing when things were not going his way. He wound up retiring, but because he did so when he was down 7-5, 3-0 rather than sticking out the match, he was booed by the crowd.

Norrie expressed sympathy for Kyrgios and mused about just how much the Australian wonder could accomplish if he remained fully healthy.[xv] Some watching might have added, *and fully dedicated.*

The rest of the schedule leading up to the U.S. Open did not go much better. Kyrgios lost to #195 Stan Wawrinka in the first round of the Toronto Masters 1000. He scored nice wins over #77 Denis Kudla and #21 Borna Coric at the Cincinnati Masters 1000 but was then beaten by missile-hitting Juan Martin del Potro, who had climbed to #3 in the world.

Down to #30 in the world, Kyrgios won two matches at the U.S. Open before coming up against Roger Federer. The two had typically played very competitive matches up to this point, but on this occasion, Federer blasted past the Aussie, winning 6-4, 6-1, 7-5.

Something about that match seemed to just about do Kyrgios in for the 2018 season. He lost again to

Federer at the Laver Cup following the U.S. Open. He then traveled to Asia for the late-season hard-court swing and went just 2-3 across tournaments in Tokyo, Shanghai, and Moscow. In Shanghai, a chair umpire once again suggested that Kyrgios was not giving a professional effort. And in the last loss, Murray had to withdraw to nurse his still-ailing elbow.

Kyrgios finished the season 25-14, his ranking having fallen to #35 in the world. Persistent injuries and his questionable commitment to the sport had finally caught up to his play.

That said, and to his immense credit, Kyrgios revealed in the weeks following the end of his season that he had begun seeing psychologists to assist with his mental health.[xvi] Stating openly that he was "trying to get on top of" his mental health, Kyrgios even added, "I probably left it too long. But I've been doing that and I feel more open about talking about it, I don't feel like I've got to hide that sort of stuff anymore." With some optimism, he also noted, "I think when everything lines up in my life, tennis will take care of itself."

2019

While Kyrgios was making an admirable effort to work on some of the issues that had begun to plague his career, results were not immediately apparent on the court. In fact, the 2019 season for the soon-to-be 24-year-old Australian got off to a particularly rocky start and never truly seemed to stabilize.

Kyrgios started the season with a win over Ryan Harrison in the opening round of the ATP 250 in Brisbane. He was then upset by world #40 Jeremy Chardy and subsequently fell to #52 in the rankings. Then, with a chance to regain some ground at his home Grand Slam, Kyrgios crashed out of the Aussie Open in the first round with a straight-sets loss to #17 Milos Raonic.

That early loss in Melbourne sent Kyrgios sliding to #64, and a subsequent Round of 16 loss to #82 Radu Albot at the ATP 250 in Delray Beach dropped him to #72. All of a sudden, the young phenom who had seemed to be on the cusp of storming the top 10 not long ago was slipping toward the wrong end of the top 100.

Kyrgios managed to reverse the trend somewhat emphatically at his next outing in the ATP 500 in Acapulco, however. He defeated the ever-tricky Andreas Seppi in the first round and then recovered from a first-set loss to beat #2 Rafael Nadal in three sets. Kyrgios then won two more tough three-setters against #42 Stan Wawrinka and #9 John Isner before soundly beating #3 Alexander Zverev in the final. It was Kyrgios's fifth ATP Tour title and boosted him all the way back up to #33 in the rankings.

Unfortunately, this quick recovery at Acapulco was followed by a disastrous turn at the Sunshine Double.

Kyrgios first appeared in the Indian Wells Masters 1000 only to lose 4-6, 4-6 to #39 Philipp Kohlschreiber after an opening-round bye. Then, he went to the Miami Masters 1000 where he enjoyed another bye, swept aside #131 Alexander Bublik, and crashed into a wave of controversy of his own making. Kyrgios clashed with spectators during a 6-3, 6-1 drubbing of #44 Dusan Lajovic, seeming to win the match almost as an afterthought to his own agitation. He then faced #13 Borna Coric in the Round of 16 and lost 6-4, 3-6, 2-6 while fueling all the on-court drama he could muster with his surly conduct.

Both players showed frustration in this match, but it was Kyrgios who smashed a racket to smithereens during a particularly frustrating moment. He then feigned an attempt to throw the racket only to flash a wry smile and instead hand it to a fan. When challenged about his behavior by the umpire, Kyrgios cheekily explained that he had been "folding" the racket for the fan.

That was perhaps amusing enough on its own, but overall, it was the latest in an expanding series of volatile episodes, and while Nick had calmed down after the match, he did so with fresh comments expressing doubt in his own dedication to tennis.[xvii]

"It's a tough loss. I just have to be better mentally. Simple as that," he said. However, he also noted that he had grown "bored" in the second set and that he was not built for consistent effort the way Coric might be. "It's a talent in and of itself for Coric to come in here every day and do everything to an absolute and be professional and work hard," Kyrgios said. "I don't have that … Like, we're all different."

With a chance for a fresh start on the European clay courts, Kyrgios showed up playing what can only be described as lackluster tennis. He lost in the opening round of the Madrid Masters 1000 to #49 Jan-Lennard Struff. He then scored a nice win over #14 Daniil Medvedev in the opener at the Rome Masters 1000, only to take himself completely out of the next match against up-and-coming Norwegian Casper Ruud. In that match, Kyrgios had another disruptive outburst, this time going so far as to toss a chair onto the court. He was defaulted from the tournament.

Following the debacle in Rome, Kyrgios opted to skip the French Open. This was ostensibly due to illness but may well have just been an opportunity for him to attempt to reset his season. But any attempted reset failed to manifest on the grass courts when Kyrgios returned to action.

He lost in the first round of the ATP 250 in Stuttgart and in the second at the ATP 500 at London's Queen's Club. He entered Wimbledon unseeded and ranked 43rd in the world, beating countryman Jordan Thompson in his opener before running into Rafael Nadal. Kyrgios had handled the Spanish champion well in the past but on this occasion, he lost in four sets.

Seemingly out of nowhere, Kyrgios then pieced together one of the most impressive tournament runs of his career. Playing at the annual ATP 500 in Washington, D.C., he beat American longshot Thai-Son Kwiatkowski in the first round and #33 Gilles Simon in the second. Kyrgios then beat #77 Yoshihito Nishioka and #137 Norbert Gombos each in straight sets before a clash against #6 Stefanos Tsitsipas in the semi-finals. Kyrgios prevailed in an excellent match, 6-4, 3-6, 7-6, and then won a tight, 7-6, 7-6 final over world #10 Daniil Medvedev. He had captured his sixth tour-level title and boosted his ranking back up to #27.

In keeping with the dramatically up-and-down nature of the 2019 season, though, Kyrgios then lost in the first round of the Montreal Masters 1000. Soon thereafter, he played the Cincinnati Masters 1000, beating #47 Lorenzo Sonego to start his run but then losing to #9 Karen Khachanov. During the Khachanov match, Kyrgios had another on-court meltdown. He smashed multiple rackets and criticized the chair umpire, ultimately earning a hefty fine for his actions.

At the ensuing U.S. Open, Kyrgios won just two matches before he ran into rising Russian Andrey Rublev, then ranked #43 in the world. The Australian turned in a strange performance, competing hard in the first two sets before seeming, as he sometimes did, like he lost interest. He sparked more controversy by complaining about the lights in the stadium interfering with his serve, and bizarrely lamented that the video game *Call of Duty* was "ruining" him.[xviii]

Kyrgios's tour season essentially ended there. He lost to Roger Federer in Laver Cup play after the U.S. Open and was beaten by Andreas Seppi in the first round of the ATP 250 in Zhuhai, China. Furthermore, soon after the Seppi loss, the ATP wrapped up what had been a quiet investigation of Kyrgios's conduct during the season. In late September, the association issued a fine, a 16-week suspension, and a six-month probation period to Kyrgios.

Kyrgios was able to finish 2019 on a positive note when he won two group-stage singles matches for Australia in Davis Cup play. For the year, though, he had gone just 23-15. He had won two very solid titles but had thrown as many on-court tantrums and had fallen to 30th in the ATP worldwide rankings.

2020
Perhaps reflecting his early desire to play a team sport, Kyrgios has often played some of his best and most joyous tennis in team environments. As such, it appeared to be a prudent move when he decided to start the 2020 season playing in the inaugural ATP Cup.

This was a tournament designed as a sort of replacement for the Hopman Cup and intended to become a new staple of international team competition. The tournament divided countries into group play leading to an eventual knock-out stage. Matchups were decided in a best-of-three format with each pairing competing in two singles and one doubles match.

Playing for Australia with teammates Alex de Minaur, John Millman, John Peers, and Chris Guccione, as well as former star Lleyton Hewitt captaining, Kyrgios had a strong showing. He defeated Germany's Jan-Lennard Struff and Greece's Stefanos Tsitsipas in group-stage singles matches to help Australia advance to the knock-outs.

In the quarter-finals, Kyrgios and De Minaur won a doubles tilt against Great Britain's Jamie Murray and Joe Salisbury; Kyrgios also won his singles match over Cameron Norrie. In the next round, however, Australia fell to Spain and Kyrgios lost to world #9 Roberto Bautista Agut.

It was a strong showing for the Aussies overall and set the season off on a strong note. With his ranking back up to #26, Kyrgios headed to the Australian Open and won his first match in straight sets over #53 Lorenzo Sonego. He then defeated #61 Gilles Simon 6-2, 6-4, 4-6, 7-5 to earn a Round of 32 date with #17 Karen Khachanov.

That matchup wound up producing perhaps the most gripping match of Kyrgios's career to date. The Aussie came out in fine form and won the first two sets 6-2, 7-6. Never one to quit or grow tired, Khachanov responded by winning the next two sets in tight tiebreaks. But in the deciding set, it was Kyrgios who had a little more to give. Playing some of his finest tennis in front of a roaring home crowd, he closed out the fifth set and the match with a 10-8 tiebreak.

Nonetheless, the match had not been smooth. Kyrgios had had his characteristic spats with the umpire and had also seemingly agitated one of his legs. It was also a marathon, clocking in as the longest match of the Aussie's career to that point. In the end, however, he was able to collapse on the court smiling as the Melbourne crowd cheered his success.

"It was insane," was about all he could say after a contest that *The Guardian* referred to as an "unhinged psychodrama."[xix]

Kyrgios lost his next match in four sets to #1 Rafael Nadal. But his Australian Open had still been a step in the right direction. Unfortunately, we'll never know how far this strong start to the 2020 season might have taken the volatile Aussie.

In the ATP 500 in Acapulco following the Australian Open, Kyrgios retired from his opening match with an injured wrist. Then, not long thereafter, the spread of the COVID-19 pandemic upended the season, causing tournament cancellations and delays. Kyrgios was out of action through the fall and ultimately decided not to travel to the U.S. for the U.S. Open amidst the turmoil of the pandemic. Thus, he ended the 2020 season having played only nine matches and with his ranking having dropped to 45th despite the fact that he had played strong, inspired tennis.

2021

The tennis calendar was not yet back to normal in 2021. While the U.S. Open and a delayed French Open had been held the previous fall, there were still scheduling difficulties stemming from the ongoing pandemic. Additionally, ATP, WTA, and tournament organizers were working on ways to keep events as safe and contained as possible. This meant that tournaments largely became "bubble" environments designed to minimize the potential for COVID-19 spread.

Within these bizarre circumstances, Nick Kyrgios started his season at an ATP 250 tournament being held in Melbourne to minimize travel ahead of the U.S. Open. He won his first two matches of the year against #209 Alexandre Muller and #324 Harry Bourchier. He then lost 3-6, 4-6 to #25 Borna Coric, avoiding the severe frustrations of their most recent matchup.

Kyrgios stayed in Melbourne for the Australian Open the following week. He beat #185 Frederico Ferreira Silva in the first round and then played a marathon match against Ugo Humbert. Kyrgios lost the first set 5-7, evened the match up, and then lost the third, 3-6. He came back to take the match by winning the last two sets 7-6, 6-4. It was an impressive performance but it did not spark a run. Kyrgios was beaten by #3 Dominic Thiem, who was fresh off a U.S. Open title, in the next round.

After the Thiem loss, Kyrgios seemed to simply disappear from the tour. The effects of the pandemic made for a strange-feeling season to begin with, and perhaps for this reason, the Aussie's absence received relatively little attention. Upon his return at Wimbledon in late June, though, it was made clear that he had stepped away to protect his mental health. An article at the Australian Open's official website stated that Kyrgios had had an "honest conversation with himself" and determined that competing week-to-week in bubble environments would not put him in a "good mental headspace."[xx]

Incidentally, that article was written following a first-round victory for Kyrgios. He had come out of nowhere, his ranking down to 60th in the world, to beat the same French opponent he had played in his last win back at the Australian Open. And as the article pointed out, many had doubted whether it would be possible for Kyrgios to "step off the couch," so to speak, and compete at Wimbledon.

"A lot of people were telling me there's no chance," Kyrgios said. He singled out famous coach and commentator Brad Gilbert for having told him this and said in response, "Dude, I know my game, I know how to play on grass. I'm not scared of anyone in the draw. I know if I believe and I'm feeling good mentally, like,

I know what I'm capable of." He stressed that his way of preparing worked for him, and beating the world #25 in the opening round seemed to validate the approach.

Kyrgios won his next match as well, against #77 Gianluca Mager. In the Round of 32, however, he was tied one set apiece with #19 Felix Auger-Aliassime when he had to retire due to an abdominal injury. It appeared that while Kyrgios's level had been up to Wimbledon competition, his body may not have been after an extended break. Then again, it may also just have been bad luck.

For his part, Kyrgios was "devastated" to withdraw, but had feared that he might tear a muscle if he kept serving.[xxi] Despite the disappointment, he took a positive spin on the experience. "I'm enjoying myself," he said after the match. "Going from the bad boy of tennis, all this stuff, to now one of the crowd favorites … I know they wanted me to keep playing. I tried to give everything I absolutely could."

Sadly, despite these positive comments, the abdominal injury and subsequent recovery time disrupted Kyrgios's rhythm and he struggled to find his top form for the remainder of the 2021 season.

The Aussie won his first match back on hard courts at the ATP 250 in Atlanta but then fell to #29 Cameron Norrie. This knocked him down to 77th in the ATP rankings, after which he dropped his opening-round match at the ATP 500 in Washington, D.C., to #107 Mackenzie McDonald. Kyrgios then lost to #32 Reilly Opelka in the first round of the Toronto Masters 1000, skipped the Cincinnati Masters 1000, and was booted from the U.S. Open by #21 Roberto Bautista Agut in the Round of 128. With his ranking down to 95th, Kyrgios competed in the Laver Cup in Boston but lost his round-robin match to Stefanos Tsitsipas.

Kyrgios was not necessarily to blame for his 2021 struggles. He had made a responsible decision to avoid bubble environments for his own mental well-being and had returned with a sharp game and positive attitude. Derailed by the Wimbledon abdominal injury, though, he wound up finishing the season with a 7-8 record and nearly fell out of the top 100.

Doubles Slam and Wimbledon Final

It was reasonable to expect some positive momentum for Kyrgios heading into the 2022 season. While the latter half of 2021 had been something of a disaster, the Kyrgios who had appeared at Wimbledon had seemed mature, relaxed, and—on the court—very dangerous. As it happened, though, the 2022 season started with a bit more bad luck. Kyrgios struggled with asthma when he ought to have been playing matches ahead of the Australian Open. He then came down with COVID-19, missing the entire Australian

Open tune-up season and dropping out of the top 100 in the rankings in the process.

Kyrgios still made it into the Australian Open draw and managed to win his first match against #128 Liam Broady. He faced #2 Daniil Medvedev in the second round and managed to win a set but ultimately fell short. Frankly, it was a fairly impressive showing given that the Aussie had been sick with COVID when he ought to have been getting sharp for the Grand Slam.

Even more impressive was what happened in the Australian Open doubles. Ever the fan of team sports, Kyrgios had often enjoyed playing with a partner when he had the opportunity. At the 2022 Australian Open, he paired up with his good friend and fellow Aussie, Thanasi Kokkinakis. The duo won their first two matches in straight sets before fighting through Round of 16 and quarter-final contests in three sets each. In the semi-final, Kyrgios and Kokkinakis pulled off a 7-

6, 6-4 upset over the pair of Spain's Marcel Granollers and Argentina's Horacio Zeballos, ranked #7 and #6 in doubles, respectively.

That upset brought about an all-Australian final pitting Kyrgios and Kokkinakis against Matthew Ebden and Max Purcell. By that point, there was considerable buzz surrounding the former pair. Kyrgios had never been that deep in a Slam doubles tournament, and he and Kokkinakis were unabashedly having an absolute blast together. It had begun to seem like a Slam title was destined. And sure enough, it was Kyrgios and Kokkinakis who prevailed in the final, beating their countrymen 7-5, 6-4.

"I can honestly say we didn't expect to come even close to this," Kokkinakis said of the dream title run.[xxii] "This is a crazy cherry on the top." Kyrgios added jubilantly, "I wouldn't have wanted to do this with anyone else."

Kyrgios followed this new career highlight with his best performance in the U.S. Sunshine Double in several years. He reached the quarter-final of the Indian Wells Masters 1000 and took a set from Rafael Nadal before falling just short of the upset. He then defeated #61 Adrian Mannarino, #7 Andrey Rublev, and #34 Fabio Fognini before losing to #11 Jannik Sinner in the Round of 16 at the Miami Masters 1000. These tournaments got the Aussie back into the top 100 ahead of the clay-court season.

Kyrgios skipped the bulk of that season as he sought to optimize his schedule. But he did make a semi-final run at the ATP 250 on Houston clay courts, which helped him ascend to #78 in the rankings.

Nearly two months later and now at 27 years of age, Kyrgios was back on the grass at the ATP 250 in Stuttgart, Germany. He won three matches there before losing to Andy Murray, who at #68 was attempting to return to the top of the game after a slew of devastating injuries.

At the next tournament, an ATP 500 in Halle, Germany, Kyrgios displayed compelling form. He dispatched hometown favorite Daniel Altmaier in the first round, got past #6 Stefanos Tsitsipas in the second, and then beat #19 Pablo Carreno Busta in straight sets. He lost in the semi-final to #12 Hubert Hurkacz and then had an abbreviated stay at the ATP 250 in Mallorca. Nevertheless, it was clear that Kyrgios had found his game. His ranking skyrocketed from 115th at the outset of the Australian Open to 40th.

Kyrgios lost his first set back on the Wimbledon lawns to British hopeful Paul Jubb. This led to a back-and-forth match during which the Australian flirted with disaster before prevailing in a 7-5 fifth set. He righted the ship in the next round, though, with a 6-2, 6-3, 6-1 blitz of #31 Filip Krajinovic. Then, Kyrgios made a statement with a four-set win over #5 Stefanos Tsitsipas.

In the Round of 16, he had another brush with disaster, losing the first and fourth sets in a match with talented American Brandon Nakashima. Once again, though, Kyrgios was able to prevail in a fifth set. He advanced to the quarter-finals where he defeated #43 Cristian Garin.

This would have set up a semi-final with Rafael Nadal, but the Spaniard was forced to withdraw with an injury, paving the way for Kyrgios to play in his first-ever Grand Slam final. In that final, Kyrgios took the first set from world #3 Novak Djokovic. But from there he lost the next three, falling just short of a singles Grand Slam triumph.

The defeat left Kyrgios understandably disappointed. However, he was also positive, saying after the match, "I felt like I belonged, to be honest."[xxiii]

Djokovic, with his 21st Grand Slam trophy in hand, seemed to agree, telling Kyrgios, "Everything is starting to come together for you."

It certainly felt as if Djokovic had hit the nail on the head. The vibe was that while Kyrgios may have missed his best opportunity at Grand Slam glory, he had proven he could get there one day.

Almost as impressive as the Wimbledon run itself was the fact that Kyrgios then backed it up with a tournament victory at the ATP 500 in Washington, D.C. This had become a favorite tournament over the years, and in 2022, the Aussie had to get past three top-35 Americans on their home soil to win it. He did just that, and then swept past #115 Mikael Ymer and #96 Yoshihito Nishioka in the semis and final.

Kyrgios continued his impressive play at the Montreal Masters 1000. While he was knocked out in the quarter-final by #10 Hubert Hurkacz, he managed to beat world #1 Daniil Medvedev and #21 Alex de

Minaur, his fellow Australian, along the way. He was less successful at the next Masters 1000 in Cincinnati but had still done enough on the hard-court swing to raise his ranking to #25 heading into the U.S. Open.

In New York, Kyrgios had to play against Thanasi Kokkinakis in the first round. He beat his good friend in straight sets (though the two would continue to play doubles together and make it to the Round of 16 at the same tournament). Kyrgios then won in four sets against #50 Benjamin Bonzi and in straights against upstart American J.J. Wolf. In the Round of 16, he defeated #1 Daniil Medvedev again and for a moment, it seemed as if he might get himself right back into a Slam final. In the quarter-final, however, Kyrgios was stopped by #31 Karen Khachanov in five sets.

The U.S. Open helped Kyrgios back into the top 20. From there, he played only one more tournament in 2022: the ATP 500 in Tokyo. He won two matches before withdrawing from a clash with #11 Taylor Fritz due to a knee injury.

At the end of a remarkable comeback season, Kyrgios was 37-10 and #22 in the world. He had won the Australian Open in doubles, seized a singles title, and perhaps best of all, he had looked happy doing it!

Recurring Injuries

Kyrgios withdrew from the earliest 2023 tournaments to allow minor injuries to heal. There was no concern about his availability for the Australian Open, however, and there had never been more hype. The Aussie's 2022 season had convinced the tennis world all over again that his best days may yet be ahead of him, and thus, he was seen as a potential favorite in Melbourne.

On the eve of the tournament, the *New York Times* published a piece titled, "Nick Kyrgios Is Coming For Tennis."[xxiv] The article examined Kyrgios's evolution from a "temperamental talent with so much unrealized potential" into "the sport's biggest draw," still something of a bad boy but more performer than disruptor. Indeed, a *good* Kyrgios who was animated but, for the most part, focused, had become one of the sport's main attractions.

Beyond that, though, the *Times* article noted that Nick was also taking his game more seriously. It revealed that he had spent much of 2022 focusing on his nutrition and training in a way he had seldom done before. He was also in a clearer mental space, feeling less alone than he had at times in his career, and more able to open up to people. The prevailing takeaway was that he *was* finally realizing his potential, and what was more, acting on it. It felt like he might be on the cusp of something great.

"Tennis, like few other sports, is an M.R.I. of the soul," the *Times* said. And Kyrgios's soul had seemingly never been in a healthier place since he turned professional.

But sadly, it was precisely then that disaster struck. Fully expected to compete in the Australian Open and potentially contend for a title, Kyrgios had to withdraw from the tournament at the last second. A knee injury had come up out of the blue and there was a need for arthroscopic surgery.

Nick had the surgery and sat out the early hard-court season recovering and rehabbing. He initially hoped to return to the tour for the clay-court season. But then he underwent an unexpected and scary ordeal when an armed robber held up his mother and stole Kyrgios's Tesla. During the incident, according to Kyrgios's agent, the Aussie cut his foot. The injury was bad enough to keep him off the court through the clay season. Thankfully, however, no greater harm was done to him or his family.

Kyrgios returned at the ATP 250 in Stuttgart and lost to world #64 Yibing Wu. He subsequently set about getting ready for Wimbledon but, in the process, he tore a wrist ligament. This effectively ended the 2023 season for Kyrgios, and he proved unable to return early in 2024 either.

As of this writing, Nick Kyrgios has not played a professional match since that loss in Stuttgart. He has fallen completely out of the world rankings and suddenly, there are some who believe he may consider retirement. Kyrgios himself has been somewhat ambiguous on the issue.

In December of 2023, he said on a podcast, "If it was up to me, I don't really want to play anymore, to be honest."[xxv] But he added, "I have to almost [keep playing]. I've got so much more to give but, for me, I don't feel like playing anymore."

Chapter 4: Kyrgios the Commentator

What happened to Nick Kyrgios in 2023 was terrible. He had caught a groove in 2022 and seemed to be in the healthiest place mentally he had been throughout his entire career. He was also playing wonderful tennis and making great progress in the sport's biggest events. But the injuries came suddenly. Sometimes, the world of professional sports is simply that cruel.

Whether or not Kyrgios makes it back to where he was heading into the 2023 season, though, there is something of a silver lining in his absence from the tour, and that is that he quickly emerged as a fresh talent as a tennis commentator.

This began at the ATP Finals in 2023 when Kyrgios joined Tennis Channel for some on-air work. Because the ATP Finals is a brief event, this work amounted to just five days at the Tennis Channel desks. In that time, however, Nick demonstrated both a deep knowledge of the game and a knack for communication.

Regarding the former, it was fascinating for fans to hear a player not just speaking with the experience of a professional but offering unbiased insights on his own opponents and rivals. As for the latter, Kyrgios simply proved to have an easy way about him on air; while there were hints of the irreverence and lack of seriousness we've often seen from him on the court, he tempered his approach with a laid-back quality that was both calming and enjoyable. Among tennis fans and even media members, there seemed to be almost universal approval of Kyrgios's commentary.

With the ATP Finals coverage having gone so well, Kyrgios also joined ESPN to do Australian Open coverage once his knee injury arose in Melbourne in early 2024. He was a natural complement to longtime commentators such as Chris Fowler, John McEnroe, and others. Fans and media alike responded favorably. As *The Telegraph* put it, "Nick Kyrgios is a TV triumph," as "shrewd" and "instructive" as he is naturally engaging.[xxvi]

At this point, we don't know if or when Kyrgios will be back on the tour. It is clear, however, that either in the interim or once he has retired, there is an appetite for more of his contributions in the booth.

Kyrgios himself appears to be well aware of this. He has already made an effort to establish his own channels for commentary through a handful of different podcast and talk-show projects. Most recently, he teamed up with WTA star Naomi Osaka's media outfit, Hana Kuma, to set up a video podcast called *Good Trouble*. In this series, he will interview fellow athletes, media members, and assorted celebrities (including former boxer Mike Tyson and super-chef Gordon Ramsay).

Speaking on potential next steps after his playing career comes to an end, Kyrgios has appeared to be open to the idea of making tennis commentary more regular as well. "I could travel the world making really good money commentating on the sport, doing things like I am now with my talk show…" he was quoted as saying in January of 2024.[xxvii]

Based on Kyrgios's work at the 2023 ATP Tour Finals and the 2024 Australian Open, the sport would be lucky for him to consider this post-career path. So, regardless of if he opts to show up with a microphone or a tennis racket in hand, one thing is certain. We have not seen the last of Nick Kyrgios yet.

Chapter 5: Nick Kyrgios's Top Rivals

From a rivalry standpoint, Nick Kyrgios has had an unusual career. For someone who has been around on the pro tour for roughly a decade, he does not have many opponents against whom he's played particularly often. This is partly because he missed a fair amount of time over the years, and partly due to the fluid and unpredictable nature of tennis draws.

The other peculiar thing about Kyrgios and his rivals is that he spent a good chunk of his career beating players he was not expected to beat and losing to others he might have been expected to compete with. For instance, he is one of very few players to have a winning head-to-head record against Novak Djokovic, but he could only solve Andy Murray once in seven tries, and he's 4-1 against Stefanos Tsitsipas, a contemporary who has had a far more consistent career than Kyrgios. Plus, he's 2-6 against Richard Gasquet, who was already entering his veteran years when the

Aussie first emerged. There is simply something topsy-turvy about how Kyrgios has handled the opponents he has seen most frequently on the tour.

Beyond those somewhat unusual pairings, though, there are a few players against whom Kyrgios has had more sustained and compelling rivalries. Three that stand out in particular are Rafael Nadal, Alexander Zverev, and Milos Raonic.

Rafael Nadal

Not counting the 2022 Wimbledon Championships when Nadal withdrew from their much-anticipated semi-final with an injury, these two have played each other nine times. That is the most matches Kyrgios has played against any opponent in his career. And while Nadal leads the head-to-head by a tally of 6 to 3, Kyrgios's wins have come in particularly big moments; after all, the most memorable match they played was Kyrgios's breathtaking Wimbledon breakthrough back in 2014. The Aussie upended the

Spanish legend 7-6, 5-7, 7-6, 6-3 on that occasion, effectively announcing himself to the tennis world as an emerging heavyweight contender at Grand Slam events.

Beyond the head-to-head numbers and match results, the nature of the Kyrgios/Nadal rivalry has also been fascinating over the years. The fact of the matter is that not many players have ever been able to compete with Nadal on pure athleticism and physicality. The Spanish champion dominated matches with his body in a way that his own greatest rivals have never quite done.

Kyrgios was a different player, to be sure, relying far more on a powerful serve and a long, rangy frame (one that no doubt played into his natural attraction to basketball, where "length" and wingspan are increasingly prized). He was also a supremely gifted athlete, and, as a result, has been able to counter Nadal with a certain physicality that others did not possess.

With Nadal creeping toward retirement and Kyrgios's status on tour uncertain in the early stages of 2024, we've likely seen the last of this rivalry. But the pairing has made for one of the more interesting matchups of the last decade.

Alexander Zverev

Nick Kyrgios's talent is such that he transcended his own generation in some ways. Fans took note of his clashes with the likes of Nadal, Djokovic, and Murray despite the fact that the Aussie never came close to matching those legends' consistency let alone their accomplishments. While those clashes have been the headline moments of Kyrgios's career, he has also had rivalries with players of his own generation as well.

Like Kyrgios, Alexander Zverev was identified very early in his career as a player with top-10 potential and the talent to win Grand Slams. The tall and tireless German emerged on a similar timeline and quickly rose toward the upper ranks of professional tennis.

Unsurprisingly, given the somewhat similar starts to their careers, Kyrgios and Zverev have met fairly frequently, with Kyrgios ultimately holding a 4-3 head-to-head edge as of this writing. Though Zverev has been a far more consistent player in general, their matchups, not unlike Kyrgios's tests against Nadal, seemed to bring out the best in the Aussie's physicality. Zverev is a fit, talented player with physical length to rival Kyrgios's and has a surprising ability to cover the court despite his 6'6" height. He demands both athleticism and versatile shot-making from his opponents, and Kyrgios meets those challenges better than most.

While Kyrgios and Zverev have never met in a Grand Slam, two of Kyrgios's four wins in the head-to-head have come at Masters 1000 events. These wins were at successive tournaments in Indian Wells and Miami during the 2017 Sunshine Double.

Milos Raonic

Milos Raonic emerged on the ATP Tour several years before Kyrgios. The two are contemporaries, however, in the sense that both have been burdened by "next-gen" expectations. The seemingly never-ending search for the next all-time great to follow in the Big Three's footsteps led to lofty projections for both of these men's careers.

Unlike Nadal and Zverev, Raonic did not push Kyrgios athletically. He was a less mobile player who relied less on reach and court coverage. Nevertheless, there was a physical component to their contests that made them quite compelling. In this case, that physical component came from the fact that few men on tour in the past decade have served as hard as well as consistently as Raonic and Kyrgios. Indeed, both players have topped 140 mph, which these days is something of a benchmark of a truly powerful serve.

To date, Raonic's slightly bigger serve has been the difference in the rivalry. While the Canadian leads the head-to-head just 4-3, he has a 3-1 edge across four meetings in Grand Slams. In the best-of-five-set Grand Slam format, the relentless power of the Raonic serve has outlasted the athleticism and versatility of the multi-talented Aussie.

Ultimately, it is difficult to declare one opponent or the other as Kyrgios's main career rival. As of now, it might be most logical to point to Nadal simply due to the memorable nature and quality of their matches. If Kyrgios returns to the pro tour, however, and if Zverev and Raonic can also stay healthy, both of these contemporaries will likely wind up having played Kyrgios at least as many times as Nadal did. They will likely go down as his most consistent and long-standing rivals, even if the match-ups he will be most remembered for will be those against the Big Three that loomed above him.

Chapter 6: Personal Life

Nick Kyrgios's personal life starts with his family. Through all his years traveling on the pro tour, and through the various struggles he has had as a tennis player, Nick has remained close to his parents. While they are not fixtures on the ATP Tour the way, say, Rafael Nadal's Uncle Toni or Andy Murray's mother Judy have been, they have appeared in Nick's player box on numerous occasions. This is true of Nick's sister as well. He is said to have been estranged from his brother Christos in recent years, though there are limited details available about the state of that relationship now.

Romantically, Nick is known to have been involved with a few women since becoming a public figure. First among his known partners was Ajla Tomljanovic, herself a pro tennis player from Australia. The two dated during the mid-2000s and even played mixed doubles together at the Australian Open in 2016. They did not get out of the first round together, but the experience appears to have laid a foundation for friendship through tennis. Though Kyrgios and Tomljanovic split up around 2017, they have hit together in tournament practice on occasion since then. By all accounts, the two seem friendly.

In late 2021, meanwhile, Nick started dating a woman named Costeen Hatzi. Hatzi is an interior designer and influencer on social media who graduated from Australian Catholic University with a degree in psychological sciences. Thanks in part to the fact that she featured heavily in Kyrgios-centric portions of Netflix's *Break Point* tennis documentary, we know quite a lot about her and how she views the relationship. The simple truth seems to be that they make one another better.

According to Kyrgios's manager and friend Daniel Horsfall, past girlfriends have not necessarily had a positive impact on Nick. By contrast, Hatzi "lifts him up and gives him motivation and inspiration."[xxviii]

For his part, Kyrgios has said, "You know, I'm fortunate enough to be in a really healthy relationship that's loving, she supports me, and we just have fun."

The two are not engaged yet as of this writing, but there have been some rumors suggesting they could make things official before much longer.

Outside of his family and relationships, Nick Kyrgios has typically filled his personal life with sports. This might not typically be worth noting given how many people around the world would count sports as a primary hobby or interest. Kyrgios, though, is known to be a particularly obsessive sports fan with a deep interest in his favorite teams and leagues that goes beyond a casual hobby.

While the tennis star is known to be a longtime supporter of London-based soccer club Tottenham Hotspur, he is most closely associated with the NBA's

Boston Celtics. Kyrgios follows the team extremely closely, occasionally wearing Celtics jerseys to warm up before tennis matches and even going so far as to credit certain Celtics results with his play on a given day.

Locally, meanwhile, Kyrgios is also a supporter of the National Rugby League's Canberra Raiders, his home team, and the Australian Football League's North Melbourne FC. He also has ownership stakes in two sports organizations: the National Basketball League's South East Melbourne Phoenix and the Miami Pickleball Club.

Even though Nick spends a great deal of time on his sports-related interests, he also finds ways to do good. He has been associated with a handful of charitable efforts over the years. Perhaps the most notable of these was his effort to rally relief following the 2019 and 2020 bushfires in Australia. These horrific fires devastated Australian wildlife, nature, and human populations, but gained more attention than they otherwise might have because they affected early-2020 tennis tournaments in the country. Having seen firsthand the effects of the fires on his hometown of Canberra, Kyrgios announced that he would donate money to relief efforts for every ace he hit in tennis. This led to others following suit, and, in a sense, snowballed into the "Rally for Relief" effort in which prominent tennis stars raised significant sums to help. Kyrgios stressed that he did not do this for media attention, but that he knows he commands that attention anyway, and used the fact to try to reach more people about the fires.[xxix]

Aside from the isolated but severe incident of the bushfires, Kyrgios has primarily focused his philanthropic efforts on the establishment of The Nick Kyrgios Foundation. This is an organization that seeks to improve young people's access to sports.

Last but not least, it also has to be mentioned that Kyrgios has unofficially become a crucial influencer with regard to mental health. Fortunately, there has been something of a trend of major sports figures speaking out about their own mental health issues throughout the 2010s and into the 2020s. Names like Olympic gymnast Simone Biles, tennis star Naomi Osaka, and NBA standout Kevin Love all come to mind as figures who have sparked important discussions in this space. What makes Kyrgios particularly important, however, is that his struggles have been visible.

Fans have watched over the years as Kyrgios struggled with his emotions and mental state on the tennis court. Plenty of players are feisty or heated in dramatic moments, but Kyrgios has been temperamental and unpredictable in the extreme at times. Indeed, there were days when it seemed his greatest rival was *himself.*

Yet, we have also seen Nick become somewhat more measured over time—still fiery and capable of an outburst, but less likely to display radical mood swings or prolonged unprofessional behavior. Furthermore, we can directly connect the positive change in his demeanor to his concerted efforts to improve his mental well-being, as he has publicly discussed those efforts.

This is not to suggest that we, as viewers, can pinpoint exact moments when Kyrgios's mental health diligence has paid off on the court. We can, however, recognize a man who has freed himself of the stigma of mental health difficulties, worked to address problems, and seen positive trends as a result. This is an invaluable lesson for fans of all ages who have watched Nick Kyrgios over the years.

Chapter 7: Legacy

Nick Kyrgios is, at the time of this writing, only about a decade into his professional career. He eased onto the tour throughout the 2014 season and has yet to play a match in 2024. Once upon a time, that would have been a fairly ordinary length for a professional tennis player's career. These days, however, it would be a short tenure for a high-level player.

This is simply to suggest that Kyrgios may well have a lot of years of tennis left in front of him. While it is true that he has had serious injuries in recent years, we have seen him recover swiftly and completely before. Furthermore, while Kyrgios has openly questioned whether he wants to continue playing tennis, his dedication has also been a fluid matter over the years. No one should presume to know Kyrgios's state of mind, but it would be in keeping with his character and tendencies for him to have said he no longer wanted to play simply because that was what he was feeling in the moment. But when he is feeling healthy and one of his favorite parts of the calendar is approaching—say, the grass-court season in 2024 or the Australian Open in 2025—he may well begin to feel differently.

Naturally, Kyrgios stands to alter the nature of his legacy if he does return to the sport. Particularly, if he returns with the form and poise he showed late in 2022, there may yet be significant accomplishments around the corner for the still-young Aussie. It is even conceivable, though perhaps not likely, that Nick Kyrgios will still find his way into the Grand Slam club in singles one of these years. But right now, we simply don't know.

At this stage, however, if he never plays another match, Kyrgios has already pieced together a fascinating legacy. He will be remembered first and foremost as a titanic talent. Kyrgios is a rare athlete, even in the ranks of professional tennis, and he developed his game to the point that he could regularly compete with and beat the best players in the world. In the opening minutes of Netflix's *Break Point* episode titled "The Maverick," former top-10 player Matteo Berrettini and legendary player and commentator John McEnroe suggested that Kyrgios is the most talented player of his generation.[ii]

In keeping with those comments, there has always been a sense that, had everything gone right for him, Kyrgios might have joined or followed the Big Three atop the ATP Tour. For those who watched him play, that sense will linger long after Kyrgios stops playing.

Unfortunately, Kyrgios will also be remembered for the negatives. First, there is the perceived lack of drive. In that same documentary episode, former U.S. Open champion Andy Roddick suggests, with a tone of disappointment, that Kyrgios treats the sport like a hobby. Later in the same episode, WTA legend Martina Navratilova laments (with a laugh) that Kyrgios can't put the same energy into singles that he did into that doubles run. These comments speak to a prevailing perception that the Aussie has almost refused to tap into his full ability.

There is also his wild temper on the court to consider. Now, there are some who regard professional tennis as being almost too polite or too proper. Many will argue that the sport *needs* players with big personalities, and that the occasional outburst serves to balance out the too-gentle-by-half culture of the sport.

These are fair perspectives, and they speak to a role that Nick Kyrgios has certainly filled at times. On many occasions, though, the Aussie has gone too far, berating officials, smashing rackets, and even arguing loudly with fans. Of course, those things only seemed to happen when matches were not going Kyrgios's way, and that makes them even more difficult to justify. There is, in the end, no way around the basic fact that Kyrgios's frequent attitude problems on the court detracted from the player he could have been.

Nonetheless, there are also plenty of fans who find this "bad boy" persona not only immensely relatable but also highly entertaining to watch.

What really ought to factor into Kyrgios's legacy in the end, though, is a combination of these memorable factors—his ability, his struggles, and the aforementioned efforts he has publicly spoken of to overcome those obstacles.

In the world of professional tennis, particularly in the 21st century, the leading figures have been demigods. Roger Federer, Rafael Nadal, and Novak Djokovic, as well as Serena and Venus Williams, simply don't seem like ordinary humans. They are infallible masters in their arenas, wonderful to watch and captivating to cheer for but, in some ways, difficult to relate to. These players are *so* good that it may even have been difficult for a young fan to tune in and say, with any sense of realism, "I want to be like them."

That is not to say that anyone should aspire to be like Kyrgios. But by being at once so spectacularly talented and so nakedly imperfect, the Aussie had a way of making the sport itself feel a little closer to the fans. He shows us what it looks like for a typical, flawed human being to flirt with the highest peaks of a sport. Granted, we don't all have Kyrgios's natural athletic or physical gifts. But the point is that we watched him struggle to make the most of those gifts, just as we all fall short, at times, of maximizing our own talents or potential.

Perhaps in the end, whether he ever plays another match or not, Nick Kyrgios's legacy should be thought of as simple. He has been one of the sport's supreme talents and one of its most flawed individuals at the same time. An utterly elite, utterly ordinary person who just so happened to pick tennis. Or, to hear him tell it, have it picked *for* him.

As for what he will ultimately accomplish in the sport, only time will tell. "I'm here to show you I'm one of the best players in the world," Kyrgios said following his doubles Grand Slam triumph at the Australian Open.[ii] Whether he has accomplished that mission is an unsettled matter. Now, the ball is in his court.

Final Word/About the Author

Wow! You made it to the end of this book, and you're reading the About the Author section? Now that's impressive and puts you in the top 1% of readers.

Since you're curious about me, I was born and raised in Norwalk, Connecticut. Growing up, I could often be found spending many nights watching basketball, soccer, and football matches with my father in the family living room. I love sports and everything that sports can embody. I believe that sports are one of the most genuine forms of competition, heart, and determination. I write my works to learn more about influential athletes in the hopes that from my writing, you the reader can walk away inspired to put in an equal if not greater amount of hard work and perseverance to pursue your goals.

I've written these stories for over a decade, and loved every moment of it. When I look back on my life, I am most proud of not just having covered so many different athletes' inspirational stories, but for all the times I got e-mails or handwritten letters from readers on the impact my books have had on them.

So thank you from the bottom of my heart for allowing me to do work I find meaningful. I am incredibly grateful for you and your support.

If you're new to my sports biography books, welcome. I have goodies for you as a thank you from me in the pages ahead.

Before we get there though, I have a question for you…

Were you inspired at any point in this book?
If so, would you help someone else get inspired too?

You see, my mission is to inspire sports fans of all ages around the world that anything is possible through hard work and perseverance…but the only way to accomplish this mission is by reaching everyone.

So here's my ask from you:

Most people, regardless of what the saying tells them to do, judge a book by its cover (and its reviews).

If you enjoyed *Nick Kyrgios: The Inspiring Story of One of Tennis' Stars,* please help inspire another person needing to hear this story by leaving a review.

Doing so takes less than a minute, and that dose of inspiration can change another person's life in more ways than you can even imagine.

To get that generous 'feel good' feeling and help another person, all you have to do is take 60 seconds and leave a review.

<u>If you're on Audible</u>: hit the three dots in the top right of your device, click rate & review, then leave a few sentences about the book with a star rating.

If you're reading on Kindle or an e-reader: scroll to the bottom of the book, then swipe up and it will prompt a review for you.

If for some reason these have changed: you can head back to Amazon and leave a review right on the book's page.

Thank you for helping another person, and for your support of my writing as an independent author.

Clayton

Like what you read?
Then you'll love these too!

This book is one of hundreds of stories I've written. If you enjoyed this story on Nick Kyrgios, you'll love my other sports biography book series too.

You can find them by visiting my website at claytongeoffreys.com or by scanning the QR code below to follow my author page on Amazon.

Here's a little teaser about each of my sports biography book series:

Tennis Biography Books: This series covers the stories of tennis greats such as Serena Williams, Rafael Nadal, Andy Roddick, and more.

Basketball Biography Books: This series covers the stories of over 100 NBA greats such as Stephen Curry, LeBron James, Michael Jordan, and more.

Football Biography Books: This series covers the stories of over 50 NFL greats such as Peyton Manning, Tom Brady, and Patrick Mahomes, and more.

Baseball Biography Books: This series covers the stories of over 40 MLB greats such as Aaron Judge, Shohei Ohtani, Mike Trout, and more.

Basketball Leadership Biography Books: This series covers the stories of basketball coaching greats such as Steve Kerr, Gregg Popovich, John Wooden, and more.

Soccer Biography Books: This series covers the stories of tennis greats such as Neymar, Harry Kane, Robert Lewandowski, and more.

Women's Basketball Biography Books: This series covers the stories of many WNBA greats such as Diana Taurasi, Sue Bird, Sabrina Ionescu, and more.

Lastly, if you'd like to join my exclusive list where I let you know about my latest books, and gift you free copies of some of my other books, go to **claytongeoffreys.com/goodies**.

Or, if you don't like typing, scan the following QR code here to go there directly. See you there!

Clayton

References

[i] Kumar, Aishwarya. "The Brilliance And Belligerence Of Nick Kyrgios". *ESPN*.com. 12 January 2023. Web.

[ii] "The Maverick." *Break Point*, directed by Martin Webb, Season 1, Episode 1, Box To Box Films, 13 January 2023. *Netflix*.

[iii] "Kyrgios Wins Osaka Mayor Cup". *Tennis.com.au*. 30 October 2012. Web.

[iv] Tuxworth, Jon. "The Next Big Thing: Kyrgios Ready To Be A Star". *Brisbanetimes.com.au*. 26 January 2013. Web.

[v] Reed, Betsy. "French Open: Nick Kyrgios Brushes Past Radek Stepanek". *TheGuardian.com*. 27 May 2013. Web.

[vi] Nguyen, Courtney. "Nick Kyrgios, 18, Turns Heads With Precocious Play At Australian Open". *SI.com*. 16 January 2014. Web.

[vii] "Kyrgios Saves Nine Match Points In Five-Set Comeback Win Over Gasquet". *Tennis.com*. 26 June 2014. Web.

[viii] Mitchell, Kevin. "Nick Kyrgios Stuns Rafael Nadal With Four-Set Wimbledon Victory". *TheGuardian.com*. 1 July 2014. Web.

[ix] Newbery, Piers. "Australian Open: Andy Murray Beats Nick Kyrgios In Last Eight". *BBC.com*. 27 January 2015. Web.

[x] Nguyen, Courtney. "Nick Kyrgios Stuns Roger Federer On Wild Day At the Madrid Open". *SI*.com. 6 May 2015. Web.

[xi] "Nick Kyrgios Beats Marin Cilic At Open 13 To Win First Career Title". *USAToday.com*. 21 February 2016. Web.

[xii] Knowlton, Emmett. "21-Year-Old Australian Tennis Player Nick Kyrgios Got Into An Argument With A Fan And Blatantly Tanked A Match". *BusinessInsider.com*. 12 October 2016. Web.

[xiii] "Nick Kyrgios Defeats Novak Djokovic In Mexican Open Upset". *TheGuardian.com*. 3 March 2017. Web.

[xiv] Harwitt, Sandra. "Nick Kyrgios After U.S. Open Loss: 'I'm Not Dedicated To The Game At All'". *USAToday.com*. 30 August 2017. Web.

[xv] Pavey, James. "Nick Kyrgios Booed Off The Court After Retiring Hurt At Atlanta Open". *SportingNews.com*. 28 July 2018.

[xvi] "Nick Kyrgios Using Psychologists To 'Get On Top Of Mental Health'". *ESPN.com*. 7 November 2018. Web.

[xvii] Bodo, Peter. "Smashed Rackets And Obscenities: The Full Nick Kyrgios Experience". *ESPN.com*. 26 March 2019. Web.

[xviii] "Nick Kyrgios Crashes Out Of US Open, Beaten In Straight Sets By Russia's Andrey Rublev". *Abc.net*.au. 1 September 2019. Web.

[xix] Jackson, Russell. "Nick Kyrgios Beats Karen Khachanov In Australian

Open Five-Set Rollercoaster". *TheGuardian.com.* 25 January 2020. Web.

xx Trollope, Matt. "Wimbledon: "I'm Not Scared Of Anyone In The Draw," Says Kyrgios". *Ausopen.org.* 1 July 2021. Web.

xxi Johnson, Paul. "Nick Kyrgios Retires From Third-Round Wimbledon Match With An Abdominal Injury". *ABC.net.au.* 3 July 2021. Web.

xxii Nick Kyrgios, Thanasi Kokkinakis Claim Australian Open Men's Doubles Title For Another Home-Country Win". *ESPN.com.* 29 January 2022. Web.

xxiii Fendrich, Howard. "Kyrgios Showed He Belonged On Slam Stage In Wimbledon Loss". *APNews.com.* 10 July 2022. Web.

xxiv Futterman, Matthew. "Nick Kyrgios Is Coming For Tennis". *NYTimes.com.* 15 January 2023. Web.

xxv "'Tired' Nick Kyrgios Says He Doesn't Want To Play Tennis Any More". *TheGuardian.com.* 12 December 2023. Web.

xxvi Tyers, Alan. "Nick Kyrgios Is A TV Triumph – He's Not As Thick As He Looks". *Telegraph.co.uk.* 21 January 2024. Web.

xxvii Bengel, Chris. "Tennis Star Nick Kyrgios Considering Retirement After Injury-Plagued 2023: 'My Time In The Sport May Be Over'". *CBSSports.com.* 24 January 2024. Web.

xxviii Bendlin, Karli and Latimer, Jolene. "Who Is Nick Kyrgios' Girlfriend? All About Costeen Hatzi". *People.com.* 28 April 2023. Web.

xxix Singh, Anshul. ""Not Looking For Media Attention": Nick Kyrgios On His Charitable Activities In 2020". *EssentiallySports.com.* 20 October 2020. Web.

Printed in Great Britain
by Amazon

57320131R00076